THE YORKSHIRE DALES
CASTLES, COTTAGES AND COUNTRYSIDE

Arncliffe, Littondale

Evening light, Bolton Castle

INTRODUCTION

The dales of Yorkshire are remarkable for the variety of features and places of interest to be seen in them as well as for their beauty of scenery. Intersected by rivers, all of which, with the exception of the Ribble (as much a Lancashire as a Yorkshire stream) flow from the Pennine range of mountains to the Ouse, each presents a multiplicity of attractions.

The dales best known to the visitor are five in number - Airedale, Wharfedale, Nidderdale, Wensleydale and Swaledale, but into each of these dales run smaller dales, as, for instance, Malhamdale into Airedale, Littondale into Wharfedale, Coverdale and Garsdale into Wensleydale. Very often there is more beauty and more to see in the tributary dale than in the valley into which it runs. Airedale, for example, as regards its lower stretches, has long, like the valley of the Calder, been given up to industrialisation. Yet to the lover of natural beauty its chief attractions can be found in Malhamdale, beyond Skipton. The wonderful amphitheatre called Malham Cove, and the dramatic gorge known as Gordale Scar - these prove remarkable contrasts to the pastoral scenery in which the valley terminates as it spreads out towards the Westmorland border.

Wharfedale is the most accessible of all the Yorkshire dales and its beauties begin at Bolton Bridge. Thenceforward, going up the dale, on foot or otherwise, Wharfedale and its river lead through scenes of extraordinary charm and beauty. Something reveals itself with every mile traversed. Bolton Priory ranks with Fountains and Tintern for loveliness of situation - a grey ruin set on a green sward in the bend of a swirling river - and Barden Tower, set high above the Wharfe, looks over an expanse of wood, hill, and moorland whose impressiveness it would be difficult to surpass. Then come the dale villages, set far enough apart to give to each an aspect of solitude. Burnsall, notable for its fine old church and great bridge; Linton, Threshfield, Grassington, Hebden - all these out-of-the-world places have charms of their own and are worth lingering in. And as the traveller goes farther along the dale its beauty increases. Just before reaching the point where Littondale falls into Wharfedale, the gigantic mass of limestone called Kilnsey Crag overhangs the road and the river. A little farther along and the traveller must choose between two routes; one, going to the left through Littondale, takes him through Arncliffe (a most engaging and picturesque village, beautifully situated and boasting a fine church set on the bank of the river) and Litton to Halton Gill, whence by a mountain track he may climb the moorlands until he is well over 2,000 feet high and finds himself on the slopes of Pen-y-Ghent, with views on either hand which cover a vast expanse of country. If he keeps to the main road of Wharfedale, passing through the villages of Kettlewell and Buckden, he will again be faced with an alternative. Just beyond Buckden a road to the right will take him, always climbing, over the hills and moors to Wensleydale and Aysgarth; a narrow lane to the left will lead him to the tiny hamlet of Hubberholme and its ancient church.

The charms of Nidderdale begin at Pateley Bridge, where the Nidd is enclosed between narrowing uplands, and as it nears its source is lost in some of the wildest moorland scenery in the county. Above Pateley Bridge, and a little beyond Greenhow Hill, the caverns of Stump Cross are found in the midst of a vast expanse of moor which stretches north and west towards Whernside and Ingleborough; here, at Keld Houses, one is at the highest populated place in Yorkshire.

Wensleydale, ranked by many lovers of dale scenery before Wharfedale, and certainly one of the most beautiful valleys in England, begins strictly speaking, at the delightfully situated village of Wensley. Here the dale narrows and becomes even more charming and picturesque as it penetrates the surrounding hills. A little way westward, on the north bank of the river, stands the still well-preserved castle of Bolton, where Mary Queen of Scots spent the first years of her captivity in England. More interesting small towns and villages follow - Askrigg, where there are fine old houses and a remarkably impressive church; Aysgarth, famous for its waterfalls; and Hawes, from which one may turn aside to see the famous Buttertubs, curious cavities in the ground on the way from Wensleydale to Swaledale across the solitary moors. Beyond Hawes, Wensleydale proper runs into a smaller, less celebrated but scarcely less beautiful valley called Garsdale, and on the other side of the hills southward from Garsdale is the romantic Dent Dale. Both of these delightful dales run towards Sedbergh, resting amidst wonderful hill-scenery on the threshold of Westmorland and the Lake District.

Swaledale is a region of delight, redolent with a character of its own. Few towns in England, if any, form such a striking picture as Richmond presents, seen from the river-banks near Easby. Turner asserted this to be one of the finest views in Europe. The old town, dominated by the massive keep of its great Norman castle, crowns the spur of a sharply defined promontory at the foot of which winds the Swale. It forms a perfect sentinel to the dale beyond, which, the farther it recedes into the wild country near the Westmorland border, becomes more and more characteristic of its qualities of solitude and isolation. This is fine country for the walker and the Pennine Way winds through secluded Swaledale across wild moorland which is threaded by the characteristic drystone walls. Places are far apart here - there is little population in the scattered villages and hamlets and the farmsteads on the moors on either side the valley are far removed from each other. Yet there are interesting places to see and linger in; Grinton, remarkable for its fine old church, locally termed the 'Cathedral of the Dales'; Reeth, perched high on a bluff which overlooks beautiful Arkengarthdale; Muker, an excellent centre from which to turn south for the moors between Swaledale and Wensleydale, and Keld, where one comes to the end of Swaledale and, apparently, to the end of the world. Beyond this is nothing - except desolate moors, rocks, hills, and the almost unbroken solitudes amongst which lie the borders of Yorkshire and Westmorland.

BOLTON ABBEY

Bolton Abbey. Beautifully situated beside a bend in the River Wharfe stands Bolton Abbey, originally founded some three miles away but moved to this romantic setting in 1154. Although much of the building is in ruins, the nave of the great abbey church is still used as the local parish church. William Wordsworth, who first visited the area in 1807, described the scene, and the legends concerning the foundation of the abbey, in his poems "Force of Prayer" and "The White Doe of Rylstone".

Barden Tower. A fine 17th century bridge spans the River Wharfe several miles above Bolton Abbey. Near it stands Barden Tower, originally one of six lodges owned by the Lords of Skipton Castle. It was used by the keepers of a once vast forest which covered much of this area of Wharfedale in the Middle Ages. In the late 15th century Lord Henry Clifford built the tall tower which turned the lodge into a fortified manor house. It became derelict after the roof was removed in 1777 and all that now remains is a romantic ruin overlooking the river. There are splendid walks in the vicinity of Barden which offer panoramic views of mid-Wharfedale.

Bolton Woods. Upstream from Bolton Abbey, the river flows through Bolton Woods where rocks, trees and deep pools make this a delightful beauty spot. Riverside paths thread their way through the woods offering both intimate glimpses of little islands which divide the waters of the river and more dramatic scenery which culminates in the impressive Strid. Here the river pours in a dashing torrent through a narrow, but deep and dangerous, chasm. It takes its name appropriately from an old English word meaning tumult or turmoil.

WHARFEDALE

Skyreholme. Longest of the dales, Wharfedale is also the most varied, accessible and popular. In the vicinity of Skyreholme, a mile from the village of Appletreewick, the gentler face of the valley shows itself. Here a well defined track leads to the summit of 1,592 feet high Simon's Seat with its craggy outcrop known as the Hen Stones. A prominent landmark, it offers some superb views across the scenery of Upper Wharfedale.

Facing page;
Linton. Standing on the bank of the River Wharfe opposite Grassington is Linton, a delightful place of grey stone houses grouped around the village green. The river here is particularly beautiful, tumbling over rocky outcrops between thickly wooded banks. In addition to a ford and stepping stones, three bridges span Linton's little beck: a clapper bridge, a modern road bridge and an ancient packhorse bridge. About half a mile below Linton Bridge, are Linton Falls which are especially impressive after heavy rain.

Grassington. Once a centre of the lead-mining industry, Grassington is the undisputed capital of Upper Wharfedale and attracts many visitors. This charming village is a place of steep sloping streets, comfortable inns and a delightful cobbled market place. Many of the buildings date from Tudor times but there are also a few fine examples of Georgian architecture. Now converted into cottages, Grassington Theatre was the scene of several appearances in the early 1800s by the famous tragedian Edmund Kean and there is a 16th century barn where John Wesley once preached. The River Wharfe is spanned here by a handsome stone bridge, originally built in 1603 to replace a medieval wooden structure.

Kilnsey Crag. The varied and spectacular scenery of Wharfedale attracts many climbers and no feature is more challenging than the massive outcrop known as Kilnsey Crag. Among the most dramatic rock formations in England, it dominates the road between Grassington and Kettlewell and is one of the best-known landmarks in Upper Wharfedale. An old bridge over the river connects Kilnsey to Conistone, an attractive little village with a church which is believed to be the oldest in Wharfedale.

Kettlewell. The village of Kettlewell is cradled in the midst of spectacular mountain scenery beneath 2,309 feet high Great Whernside. Reached across an old stone bridge, its grey stone buildings cluster on the banks of little Cam Beck where it flows into the Wharfe. A popular centre for walkers, Kettlewell is surrounded by some of the most outstanding scenery in the Yorkshire Dales National Park and the river, tumbling past dramatic, rocky crags, is at its most attractive in this vicinity.

Upper Wharfedale. Longest of the dales, Wharfedale is also the most varied and accessible. Sitting high in the centre of the Yorkshire Dales National Park, Upper Wharfedale is a typical glacial valley with steep sides rising up from a flat floor. There is evidence of habitation here dating from the Bronze Age and for generations Buckden has been an important centre for Upper Wharfedale. The area was once a Norman hunting forest, governed by its own laws and courts, and it was also here, in days gone by, that sheep farmers brought their wool to be sold. A picturesque huddle of cottages lying beneath the steep slopes of 2,302 feet high Buckden Pike, Buckden is surrounded by fine upland walking country which offers panoramic views of the superb moorland scenery.

Arncliffe. Situated in the delightful Littondale valley, Arncliffe is a picturesque village of mellow cottages grouped around a spacious green. Although the church, which stands near the bridge over the Skirfare, has been restored and modernised, the parish dates from the 12th century. Charles Kingsley was a frequent visitor to Arncliffe and part of his famous children's book, 'The Water Babies', was written here. Near the village is a remarkable mile long limestone cliff and there are several caves in the area including one, Dowkar Bottom, where relics of early man have been discovered.

NIDDERDALE

Pateley Bridge. The gateway to Nidderdale, this ancient market town was first granted a charter by
Edward II in the 14th century. With its steep cobbled main street and quaint corners, it is popular both
as a touring centre and for walkers. From ruined St. Mary's Church, now superseded by St. Cuthbert's
in the town centre, there are fine views over the dale.

Nidderdale is one of the National Park's lesser known dales but it encompasses some remarkable scenery and, with its wild countryside, high hills and reservoirs, it is sometimes known as the 'Lake District' of Yorkshire. Flowing from its source on Great Whernside to join the River Ouse near York, the Nidd twists and winds through the valley, often doubling back on itself in great loops. The lower part of the dale contains the attractive towns of Harrogate and Knaresborough but Upper Nidderdale, shut in by mountains, is wild and lonely country. Seen here from Low Moor, looking northwards, Sigsworth *(left-bottom)* is one of many splendid areas of moorland which surround Pateley Bridge, offering fine walks up and down the dale or on the moors. One of Nidderdale's most famous natural attractions is Brimham Rocks *(left-top)*. These spectacular rock formations are a well-known local feature, formed over thousands of years by the effects of erosion and weathering. This has moulded the millstone grit into fantastic shapes which have been given names like Serpent's Head, Druid's Coffin, the Writing Desk and Dancing Bear. Now protected by the National Trust, Brimham Rocks extend over an area of 50 acres and are unique in that they are the most extensive group of formations to be found anywhere in Britain.

WENSLEYDALE

Facing page;

Bolton Castle. Surrounded by open, rolling countryside, the massive fortress of Bolton Castle is built around a quadrangle with four square towers at the corners. It dates from the late 14th century and has been described as the "climax of English military architecture". In 1568 Mary, Queen of Scots, was imprisoned here after her flight to England and her bedroom can still be seen along with the chapel and dungeon. After being beseiged by Parliamentarian forces during the Civil War, the castle was finally dismantled in 1645.

Jervaulx Abbey. This once powerful Cistercian foundation was established on this tranquil spot in the valley of the River Ure in 1156. It was completely destroyed when religious houses were dissolved by Henry VIII in the 1530s and the exact location of the Abbey Church was only rediscovered during excavations in 1805. Originally a building of great beauty, little now remains except some graceful arches and pillars.

Middleham Castle. Now a hillside village known for the breeding and training of race horses, Middleham was once the capital of Wensleydale and an important market town. Middleham Castle, which dates from Norman times, passed into the ownership of the powerful Neville family, Earls of Warwick, and later of Richard III. Much visited by royalty and nobility, it became known as "the Windsor of the North". Eventually abandoned and plundered for building stone, only the shell of the building, with its imposing Gatehouse and Keep, remains.

Askrigg. This charming, compact village has a fine Perpendicular church overlooking a small cobbled square with an old stepped market cross. Once it was the main market centre for Upper Wensleydale but a turnpike road built in 1795 diverted trade to Hawes. Some of the county's highest fells are found in the area including flat-topped Addleborough. J. M. W. Turner stayed at Askrigg while painting in the Yorkshire Dales and, more recently, it was the setting for the television series "All Creatures Great and Small".

West Burton. Dating from before the Norman conquest, this attractive village has an extensive green and market cross which testify to West Burton's former importance as a market. The village lies beside a tributary of the River Ure and nearby West Burton Falls are among a number of notable falls in Wensleydale.

Aysgarth Falls. The Yorkshire Dales National Park encompasses a wide variety of scenery from wild upland moors to delightful wooded dales and Wensleydale is one of the broadest and most fertile of the valleys. Near the tranquil little village of Aysgarth is one of Yorkshire's most memorable beauty spots where the River Ure plunges down a series of waterfalls known as Aysgarth Force. The Upper, Middle and Lower Falls make a fine spectacle especially after heavy rain.

Wensleydale near Burtersett. Wensleydale one of the broadest and most open of the Dales and its slopes are patterned with drystone walls which enclose lush pastureland watered by the River Ure. It is seen here from near Burtersett, a hamlet which lies to the east of Hawes in the shelter of fells known as Burtersett High Pasture which rise to 1,686 feet.

Hardraw Force. Less than two miles from Hawes is the hamlet of Hardraw where the dramatic waterfall known as Hardraw Force is believed to be the highest unbroken fall in Great Britain. A spectacular sight, especially after heavy rain, it cascades 100 feet over a limestone crag which overhangs so far that it is possible to stand behind the water without getting wet.

Hawes. Yorkshire's highest market town, Hawes is a bustling, greystone town which takes its name from the Anglo-Saxon word "haus" – meaning "a mountain pass". Situated on the route of the Pennine Way and surrounded by splendid mountain scenery, Hawes is an excellent centre for both walking and climbing. There are breathtaking views from the summit of the nearby fells, which are some of the county's highest at around 2,000 feet. The Dales Countryside Centre is located at Hawes and it is also here that the famous Wensleydale cheese is both stored and marketed.

SWALEDALE

Thwaite. Swaledale is one of the more remote and sparsely populated of the dales, hemmed in by thickly wooded hills. Thwaite is one of several lovely greystone villages scattered throughout the valley, surrounded by wild moorland, drystone walls and ancient hedges. The Kearton brothers, well-known naturalists and pioneers of wild life photography, were born here and it was the wild and majestic countryside of Swaledale which fostered their interest in nature.

Richmond Castle. At Richmond the River Swale tumbles over boulders and washes round the commanding rock site on which this picturesque market town is built. The great Norman Castle was begun in 1071 by Alan Rufus, a nephew of William the Conqueror. Strategically situated on a hilltop, this impressive fortress with its massive 100 feet high keep overlooks the town which is an attractive mixture of twisting cobbled lanes and open spaces.

Reeth. Situated on one of the loveliest stretches of the River Swale, Reeth is an attractive little town with inns and houses clustered around a large green. Once a centre of the local lead-mining industry, it is now a popular centre from which to explore both Swaledale and Arkengarthdale, a little valley which joins Swaledale at Reeth.

Keld. As the Pennine Way winds through secluded Swaledale, it passes the village of Keld where sheep graze on the hillsides and drystone walls snake across the fells. Encircled by hills, this is the last village in the dale, almost hidden in a little pocket of the valley. It was the Viking settlers who gave Keld its name, meaning "place by the river", and the village is a splendid centre for walks both beside the river and across the fells with their rugged gorges and dramatic waterfalls.

Gunnerside. There is a fine walk from Keld to Gunnerside beside the beck which flows down a narrow gorge on its way to join the Swale. The village is spread out at the bottom of the gorge where the valley widens and here the river is spanned by a picturesque hump-backed bridge. At one time this was the stronghold of the Viking chieftain, Gunner, who gave his name to the settlement. Although the area has a tranquil pastoral aspect today, the fells surrounding the village still show evidence of the extensive workings of the lead mining industry which was a major activity and provider of employment in Swaledale until the late 19th century.

Muker. Situated at the northern end of the Buttertubs Pass, Muker has equal access to Swaledale and Wensleydale. This is wonderful walking country and nearby the river descends from the fells in a series of delightful little falls, notably Kisdon Force on the outskirts of the village. There is evidence that the area was inhabited in Neolithic times and the little church was founded in the reign of the first Queen Elizabeth.

MALHAMDALE

Malham Cove. Malhamdale is one of the smallest dales but it is famous for its rugged limestone scenery. The spectacular curving amphitheatre of Malham Cove was created by movements of the earth which took place during the Ice Age when the area on one side of the fault line dropped away leaving a massive limestone wall more than 300 feet high and 1,000 feet wide. At one time, the River Aire flowed in a valley above the cove but now it seeps into the stone and emerges at the foot of the cliff.

Limestone Pavement, Malham. The river once raced along the valley above Malham Cove but now the water has seeped deep into the ground leaving only a dry valley leading to the Limestone Pavement. Here centuries of rain, ice and sun have riddled the flat slabs of rock with fissures and crevices. There are magnificent views of the dale from the pavement which can be treacherous to walk on, especially after heavy rain when the limestone blocks become slippery.

Janet's Foss. Malhamdale, with its spectacular scenery, is fine walking country which attracts many visitors. One route, leading from the village of Malham to Gordale, traverses a wooded gorge which is now an important conservation area owned by the National Trust. Here is Janet's Foss, an awe-inspiring cleft in the overhanging cliffs where the beck tumbles over a rocky outcrop. Mineral salts brought down by the falling water have resulted in a carpet of petrified moss beneath the overhanging trees.

Malham Village. The delightful little village of Malham, with its stone cottages and hump-backed bridge over the beck, lies at the heart of the dale and is a popular centre for walkers and other visitors drawn by the dramatic scenery in the area. There is evidence of Stone, Bronze and Iron Age settlements in the area and fossils can still be found of the sea creatures who once swam here when all this land was under water. In the past Malham has profited by the mining which was carried out in the dale but for centuries farming, and especially the rearing of sheep, has been the main activity.

Gordale Scar. Like nearby Malham Cove, this deep cleft in the overhanging cliffs is part of the North Craven Fault which extends for more than twenty miles across the landscape. Here the little Gordale Beck plunges 300 feet down the rock face in a fine twin waterfall which is impressive at all times but never more so than after heavy rain when the thundering of the water echoes back from the surrounding rocks.

Skipton Castle. The historic market town of Skipton is one of the gateways to the Yorkshire Dales. The great castle, its gatehouse flanked by huge towers, was built soon after the Norman conquest and is one of the most complete medieval fortresses in the country. It has had a long and turbulent history, being the last stronghold in the north to hold out for the Royalists during the Civil War. The attractive courtyard dates from the 15th century and contains a yew-tree which is reputed to be more than 300 years old.

RIBBLESDALE

Stainforth. The River Ribble is at its most picturesque tumbling over a series of rapids near Stainforth. The stone packhorse bridge which dates from 1670 probably replaced an earlier structure built by the monks of Sawley Abbey in the 14th century. It serves as a reminder of days gone by when Stainforth lay on one of the main stagecoach routes to the North of England.

Settle. Overlooked by the distinctive slopes of Pen-y-Ghent, Settle is a small market town situated where the River Ribble flows through a gap in the Pennines. It received its first market charter in 1249 and some interesting old buildings are preserved in its narrow streets and secluded courtyards. Among them are the Shambles, once a row of butchers' shops, which stand back from the unspoiled Market Place. Gateway to the south-western dales, Settle makes a convenient base for the walkers who flock here to explore Yorkshire's remarkable limestone scenery. It is also famous as the start of the scenic Settle to Carlisle railway line.

Horton-in-Ribblesdale. Situated on the Pennine Way in the heart of the fells, the moorland village of Horton-in-Ribblesdale is a popular centre with walkers and is also surrounded by some remarkable caves and pot-holes. St. Oswald's Church dates from the 12th century and retains a simple Norman doorway and font as well as some ancient fragments of stained glass.

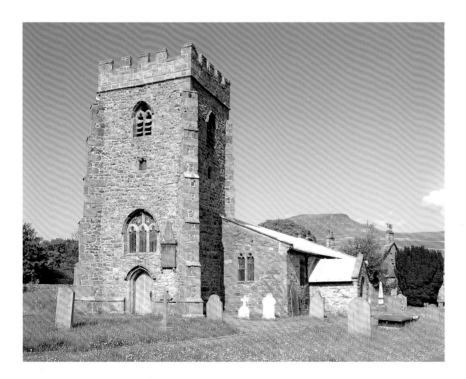

Ribblehead Viaduct. The River Ribble rises on Gayle Moor, north-east of this gigantic railway viaduct which is one of the marvels of Victorian engineering. Most famous of the twenty viaducts which were constructed along the 72 miles of the Settle to Carlisle railway line, the Ribblehead Viaduct is over 1,200 feet long and 156 feet high with twenty-four arches. Built of local stone, some of the blocks weigh more than eight tons.

Pen-y-Ghent. The famous Three Peaks, Ingleborough Fell, Whernside and Pen-y-Ghent, dominate the top of Ribblesdale near Ingleton. Although it is the lowest of the three, at 2,276 feet, Pen-y-Ghent is still impressive. Approached along the Pennine Way from Horton-in-Ribblesdale, it is popular with walkers as well as those who enjoy pot-holing and rock-climbing.

Ingleborough Fell. The country in the vicinity of Ingleton is some of the most striking in Yorkshire. Seen here from the limestone pavement, Ingleborough Fell reaches a height of 2,371 feet and forms part of the gruelling Three Peaks race. Its lower slopes are riddled with caves including one which is believed to be the largest limestone chamber in Britain. Its wealth of potholes, waterfalls and caves makes Ingleborough popular with climbers. From the top, which was the site of an Iron Age hill fort, there are panoramic views.

INGLETON AND DENTDALE

Clapham. This attractive moorland village lies midway between Ingleton and Settle. Situated at the foot of Ingleborough Fell, it is a popular centre for walkers and climbers. Rising on Ingleborough, the tumbling Clapham Beck runs through the centre of the village where it is crossed by an ancient stone bridge. Reginald Farrer, the "father of English rock gardening", was born here in 1880 and it is still possible to see remnants of some of the exotic species which he collected from all over the world.

Waterfalls Walk, Ingleton. Known far and wide for its remarkable caves and waterfalls, Ingleton is the starting point for the picturesque Waterfalls Walk which, in the course of three miles, passes no fewer than five dramatic cascades. The path traverses rugged woodland scenery which is unsurpassed anywhere in England as it meanders through the valleys of the Rivers Twiss and Doe occasionally crossing the stream by means of footbridges. The two rivers unite at Ingleton to form the River Greta which, in its turn, eventually descends through a wooded glen to join the Tees. The first falls to come into view on leaving Ingleton are the Pecca Falls *(left-bottom)*, an impressive twin cascade. At Thornton Force *(left-top)* the water tumbles more than forty feet over the overhanging limestone cliff into a pool which lies in a natural amphitheatre. Descending a steep ravine formed by the River Twiss, the remarkable Beezley Falls comprise a single fall and a spectacular triple spout. From a bridge high above the stream there are superb views of the river as it plunges down the Baxenghyll Gorge, a breathtaking wooded ravine which leads the stream on to a gentler landscape and the last waterfall in the series, the Snow Falls.

Sedbergh. Cradled between four valleys at the foot of the Howgill Fells, the historic town of Sedbergh is a popular centre poised between the Yorkshire Dales and the Lake District. The town prospered with the construction of two turnpike roads and it developed a flourishing textile industry in the 19th century. George Fox, founder of the Quakers, preached here and the Friends' Meeting House is the second oldest in England, dating from 1675.

Dentdale. One of the smallest of the dales, the enchanting valley of the River Dee is seen here from Whernside, at 2,414 feet the highest of the Three Peaks. The tree-hung river, and its tiny tributaries, run between mountains which are beginning to give way to the more rounded hills of Cumbria. The valley is characterised by its farmhouses and cottages, many of them white-washed, with the stone walls which are typical of the area snaking across the countryside.

Dent. With its old houses clustered around narrow, cobbled streets, Dent village is the main settlement in the dale. Sheep and dairy farming are the traditional activities of this somewhat isolated community but, using wool from their own sheep, the townspeople also developed a flourishing knitting industry. Restored St. Andrew's Church is believed to date from the 12th century. A drinking fountain in the centre of Dent commemorates Adam Sedgwick who was born here in 1785 and became a famous geologist and friend of Charles Darwin.

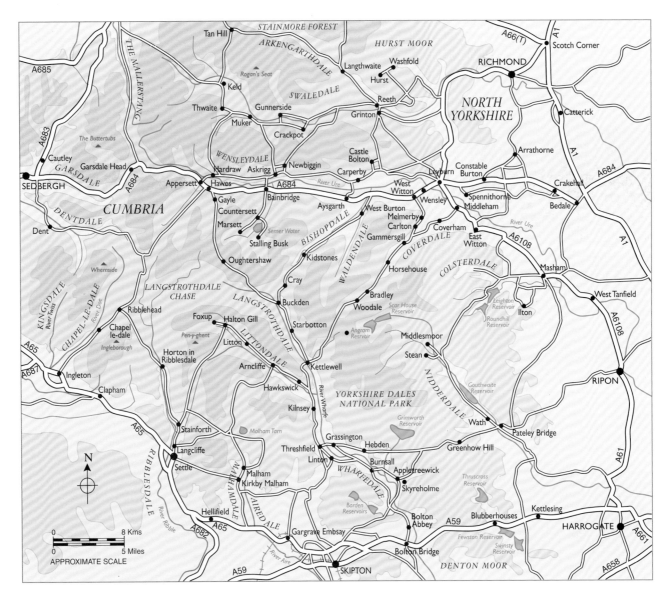

Printed and published by J. Salmon Ltd., Sevenoaks, Kent TN13 1BB
Designed by the Salmon Studio. Copyright © 2000 J. Salmon Ltd.

ISBN 1 902842 10 3

Cover picture : Buttercups near Gunnerside, Swaledale   *Back cover:* Clapham